Jada's Journey Under the Sea

Written by
Dr. Jeanette Davis

MYND MATTERS

Mynd Matters Publishing
715 Peachtree Street NE
Suites 100 & 200
Atlanta, GA 30308
www.myndmatterspublishing.com

ISBN: 978-1-953307-96-5 (pbk)

ISBN: 978-1-953307-97-2 (hdcv)

FIRST EDITION

To my Home by the Sea and the Marine
and Environmental Science Department.
Thank you for introducing me to Marine Science!

My name is Jada, and I think science is fun.
Science is cool, science is everywhere,
and science is for everyone!

There are so many sciences and so much
to explore and see. My favorite science is
the study of the ocean. It's called oceanography!

Do you ever think about what's beneath the deep, blue ocean? It has fascinating life, chemistry, and deep waves in motion!

The ocean covers about 71 percent of our planet Earth.
It's the largest habitat, so it must have value and worth.

The ocean is massive. There is so much to explore and see.
Let's take a dive and journey under the sea.

The ocean is home to unique animals and interesting creatures. And just like land, it has mountains, trenches, canyons, and many amazing features.

The plant life makes oxygen that we need to survive and breathe. They can be microscopic, growing like mats along the sea, or tall like trees.

The animals range in color and size.
There are so many to go through. But let's explore some
of the groups of ocean animals to just name a few.

Mollusks have soft bodies and are the largest group
of marine life. There are sea slugs, octopuses, squids,
oysters, and other shelled or shell-less types.

Crustaceans are arthropods with hard shells.
Some of them you may have viewed. These are crayfish,
lobsters, crabs, shrimp, and other animals we eat as seafood.

Fish are diverse. Some are jawless, and some
have skeletons made of cartilage or bone.
These include eel-shaped fish, fin fish, sharks,
and rays that are found throughout the pelagic zones.

Marine turtles are the reptiles of the sea.
There are only seven species.
There are the Flatback, Leatherback, Hawksbill, Green Turtle, Loggerhead, Kemp's Ridley, and Olive Ridley.

We can't forget the marine mammals.
Some can live on both land and sea.
These include seals, whales, dolphins,
sea otters, polar bears, and manatees.

There are many different animals that live and
thrive together in a relationship called symbiosis.
These are sponges, corals, fish, mollusks, urchins,
and others that live on reefs in closeness.

Outside of the life, the ocean has value for me and you.
It provides food, the oxygen we breathe,
and medicines when we're sick, too.

But there is not just life and other benefits under our sea.
There are also plastics, balloons, cans, bottles, and debris.

Yes, the ocean is interesting, fascinating, and fun.
We can all enjoy the ocean and beaches,
but we must be sure to clean up when we're done.

The waste causes harm to the life and chemistry in
the ocean that we need to thrive. We must stop overfishing
and polluting to keep the ocean safe and the animals alive.

We can start by reducing our waste, reusing materials,
and recycling where we can. We can plant trees,
clean beaches, and respect all life. That's the plan.

If we want the animals to thrive and use all benefits of the sea,
we must stop the pollution and leave no more human debris.

There is so much more of our ocean that hasn't
been uncovered. Let's take care of our ocean.
There is still much to discover.

Thank you, Ocean, for what you provide — the food, oxygen,
and the wonderful creatures that are wild and free.
I'll be sure to take care of you until
my next journey under the sea!

QUESTIONS TO EXPLORE THE SEA!

What are the seven species of marine sea turtles?

_____

Can you name three things that the ocean provides for humans?

_____

What's the largest group of marine life?

_____

How can we help the ocean and marine life?

_____

CPSIA information can be obtained
at www.ICGtesting.com
Printed in the USA
BVHW092005200222
629615BV00016B/375